Democratic Republic of the Congo

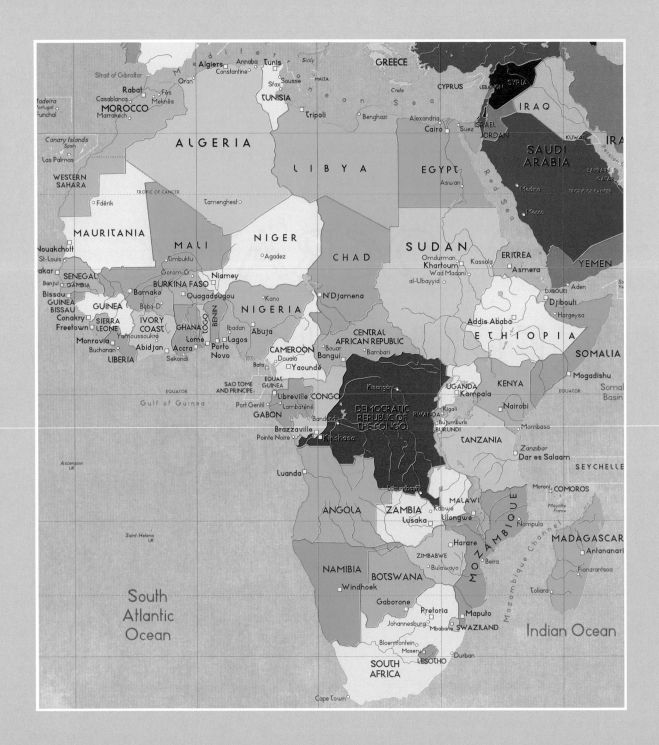

DEMOCRATIC REPUBLIC OF THE CONGO

Rita Milios

Mason Crest Publishers
Philadelphia

Produced by OTTN Publishing, Stockton, N.J.

Mason Crest Publishers
370 Reed Road
Broomall, PA 19008
www.masoncrest.com

3   5   7   9   8   6   4   2

Library of Congress Cataloging-in-Publication Data

Milios, Rita.
   Democratic Republic of the Congo / Rita Milios.
       p. cm. — (Africa)
   Includes bibliographical references and index.
   ISBN 1-59084-815-2
   1. Congo (Democratic Republic)—Juvenile literature. I. Title. II. Series.
   DT644.M55 2004
   967.51—dc22

                                            2004007113

Table of Contents

Africa: Continent in the Balance
Robert I. Rotberg

Africa is the cradle of humankind, but for millennia it was off the familiar, beaten path of global commerce and discovery. Its many peoples therefore developed largely apart from the diffusion of modern knowledge and the spread of technological innovation until the 17th through 19th centuries. With the coming to Africa of the book, the wheel, the hoe, and the modern rifle and cannon, foreigners also brought the vastly destructive transatlantic slave trade, oppression, discrimination, and onerous colonial rule. Emerging from that crucible of European rule, Africans created nationalistic movements and then claimed their numerous national independences in the 1960s. The result is the world's largest continental assembly of new countries.

There are 53 members of the African Union, a regional political grouping, and 48 of those nations lie south of the Sahara. Fifteen of them, including mighty Ethiopia, are landlocked, making international trade and economic growth that much more arduous and expensive. Access to navigable rivers is limited, natural harbors are few, soils are poor and thin, several countries largely consist of miles and miles of sand, and tropical diseases have sapped the strength and productivity of innumerable millions. Being landlocked, having few resources (although countries along Africa's west coast have tapped into deep offshore petroleum and gas reservoirs), and being beset by malaria, tuberculosis, schistosomiasis, AIDS, and many other maladies has kept much of Africa poor for centuries.

Thirty-two of the world's poorest 44 countries are African. Hunger is common. So is rapid deforestation and desertification. Unemployment rates are

The Democratic Republic of the Congo, in central Africa, is the continent's third-largest country.

often over 50 percent, for jobs are few—even in agriculture. Where Africa once was a land of small villages and a few large cities, with almost everyone engaged in growing grain or root crops or grazing cattle, camels, sheep, and goats, today more than half of all the more than 750 million Africans, especially those who live south of the Sahara, reside in towns and cities. Traditional agriculture hardly pays, and a number of countries in Africa—particularly the smaller and more fragile ones—can no longer feed themselves.

There is not one Africa, for the continent is full of contradictions and variety. Of the 675 million people living south of the Sahara, at least 130 million live in Nigeria, 67 million in Ethiopia, 55 million in the Democratic Republic of the

A painted man shows pride for his country at an international soccer match. The "Zaire" on his chest refers to the name of the Democratic Republic of the Congo before the government changed hands in 1997.

Congo, and 45 million in South Africa. By contrast, tiny Djibouti and Equatorial Guinea have fewer than 1 million people each, and prosperous Botswana and Namibia each are under 2 million in population. Within some countries, even medium-sized ones like Zambia (11 million), there are a plethora of distinct ethnic groups speaking separate languages. Zambia, typical with its multitude of competing entities, has 70 such peoples, roughly broken down into four language and cultural zones. Three of those languages jostle with English for primacy.

Given the kaleidoscopic quality of African culture and deep-grained poverty, it is no wonder that Africa has developed economically and politically less rapidly than other regions. Since independence from colonial rule, weak governance has also plagued Africa and contributed significantly to the widespread poverty of its peoples. Only Botswana and offshore Mauritius have been governed democratically without interruption since independence. Both are among Africa's wealthiest countries, too, thanks to the steady application of good governance.

Aside from those two nations, and South Africa, Africa has been a continent of coups since 1960, with massive and oil-rich Nigeria suffering incessant periods of harsh, corrupt, autocratic military rule. Nearly every other country on or around the continent, small and large, has been plagued by similar bouts of instability and dictatorial rule. In the 1970s and 1980s Idi Amin ruled Uganda capriciously and Jean-Bedel Bokassa proclaimed himself emperor of the Central African Republic. Macias Nguema of Equatorial Guinea was another in that same mold. More recently Daniel arap Moi held Kenya in thrall and Robert Mugabe has imposed himself on once-prosperous Zimbabwe. In both of those cases, as in the case of Gnassingbe Eyadema in Togo and the late Mobutu Sese Seko in Congo, these presidents stole wildly and drove entire peoples and their nations into penury. Corruption is common in Africa, and so are a weak rule-of-law framework, misplaced development, high expenditures on soldiers and low expenditures on health and education, and a widespread (but not universal) refusal on the part of leaders to work well for their followers and citizens.

Conflict between groups within countries has also been common in Africa. More than 12 million Africans have been killed in the civil wars of Africa since 1990, with more than 3 million losing their lives in Congo and more than 2 million in the Sudan. War between north and south has been constant in the Sudan since 1981. In 2003 there were serious ongoing hostilities in northeastern Congo, Burundi, Angola, Liberia, Guinea, Ivory Coast, the Central African Republic, and Guinea-Bissau, and a coup (later reversed) in São Tomé and Príncipe.

Despite such dangers, despotism, and decay, Africa is improving. Botswana and Mauritius, now joined by South Africa, Senegal, Kenya, and Ghana, are beacons of democratic growth and enlightened rule. Uganda and Senegal are taking the lead in combating and reducing the spread of AIDS, and others are following. There are serious signs of the kinds of progressive economic policy changes that might lead to prosperity for more of Africa's peoples. The trajectory in Africa is positive.

(Opposite) Women carry sticks from the dense forest near Virunga National Park, on the Democratic Republic of the Congo's eastern border. Tropical rain forest covers much of the country. (Right) A section of rapids in the Congo River, the world's fifth-longest river and a significant source of drinking water.

1 Forest and Woodland

DEEP IN THE heart of Africa, a dense tropical rainforest has existed unchanged for thousands of years. Home to exotic animals and diverse cultures, this forest makes up much of a large African country called the Democratic Republic of the Congo, formerly known as Zaire.

Sitting on the equator in central Africa, the Democratic Republic of the Congo covers 905,563 square miles (2,345,410 square kilometers), 77 percent of which is forest and woodland. It is the third-largest country in Africa, after Sudan and Algeria. Nine countries border the Congo (in this book, "Congo" will refer to the Democratic Republic of the Congo). To the south are Angola and Zambia; to the west is the Republic of the Congo (formerly Middle Congo); to the north are the Central African Republic and Sudan; and sitting along the eastern border are Tanzania, Uganda, Burundi, and Rwanda. There

11

is also a coastal area, only 23 miles (37 km) wide, on the western border touching the Atlantic Ocean.

Only 3 percent of the land in the Congo is *arable*, though most Congolese still survive by farming. They cut and burn trees from the forest in order to plant crops such as bananas, *cassava*, cocoa, coffee, corn, and palm oil. The country's vast landscape is rich in other natural resources, including copper, cobalt, gemstones, diamonds, silver, coal, iron ore, and timber.

A Variety of Climates and Landscapes

Several large rivers break up the Congo's landscape and provide a much-needed means of navigation through dense grasses, weeds, and bamboo. The Ubangi and Bomu Rivers flow through the northern part of the country. The Congo River, the world's fifth-longest river, flows north and west. It turns slightly south just before emptying into the Atlantic Ocean.

The country has three distinct climate regions. Along the eastern and southeastern borders of the Congo are ranges of plateaus and mountains. Several plateau peaks stand 6,000 feet (1,830 meters) above sea level. This region is dense with forest and plant life, and daytime temperatures average a comfortable 70°F (21°C). The average annual rainfall is about 48 inches (122 centimeters).

Savannas are the dominant feature of the southern region. This region primarily contains grassland, although some small trees do appear, mostly in the valleys. For several months at a time, the savanna will receive only small amounts of rain. The average annual rainfall level is 37 inches (94 cm).

The third climate region of the Congo is the tropical rain forest in the

Quick Facts: The Geography of the Democratic Republic of the Congo

Location: Central Africa, northeast of Angola

Area: slightly less than one-fourth the size of the U.S.
- *total:* 905,328 square miles (2,345,410 sq km)
- *land:* 875,293 square miles (2,267,600 sq km)
- *water:* 30,035 square miles (77,810 sq km)

Borders: Angola, 1,560 miles (2,511 km); Burundi, 145 miles (233 km); Central African Republic, 980 miles (1,577 km); Republic of the Congo, 1,497 miles (2,410 km); Rwanda, 135 miles (217 km); Sudan, 390 miles (628 km); Tanzania, 285 miles (459 km); Uganda, 475 miles (765 km); Zambia, 1,199 miles (1,930 km); coastline, 23 miles (37 km)

Climate: tropical; hot and humid in equatorial river basin; cooler and drier in southern highlands; cooler and wetter in eastern highlands; north of Equator—wet season April to October, dry season December to February; south of Equator—wet season November to March, dry season April to October

Terrain: vast central basin is a low-lying plateau; mountains in east

Elevation extremes:
- *lowest point:* Atlantic Ocean, 0 feet
- *highest point:* Pic Marguerite on Mont Ngaliema (Mount Stanley), 16,765 feet (5,110 meters)

Natural hazards: periodic droughts in south; Congo River floods (seasonal); in the east, in the Great Rift Valley, there are active volcanoes

Source: CIA World Factbook, 2003.

north, where the country straddles the equator. Thick forest is common in this region, and in some areas it is so dense that sunlight almost never reaches the ground. The average daytime temperature is 90°F (32°C), and the region receives about 80 inches (203 cm) of rain per year. Thunderstorms are frequent and intense though they only last for a short time. Most of the rains fall during the wet season, which in this region lasts from May to October.

Rivers, Lakes, and Mountains

In central Congo, the Congo River and its *tributaries* are the sources of two great basins that supply the country with much of its water. The Congo River branches off to create the Ubangi and Aruwimi Rivers going north and the Lomami and Kasai Rivers going south. The great river and its tributaries also serve as major transportation routes. Floating riverboats act as taxis in this land so dense with vegetation and forest that few roads can be built.

The Congo River is 10 miles (16 km) wide at its broadest point and it flows for 2,900 miles (4,667 km). It is the second-longest river in Africa, after the Nile, and crosses the equator two times. The river is home to more than 4,000 islands, many of which are used by local fishermen. It is also filled with numerous species of fish as well as other water creatures like snakes and crocodiles. Green grasses and marshes are abundant along the riverbanks.

The river is divided into four parts—the *headwaters* and the upper, middle, and lower Congo. The headwaters, where the river starts, are located in the southern part of the Congo, at the intersection of the Lualaba and Luapula Rivers. The river flows north from here until it reaches Boyoma Falls (formerly Stanley Falls), 30 miles (50 km) north of the equator. The waterfall descends from a height of 1,520 feet (460 meters) above sea level to a spot just above Kisangani, one of the country's largest cities. This section of the river, which contains many swift rapids, is the upper Congo.

The middle section of the Congo River curves northwest then turns west before going southwest, at the point where it is joined by the Ubangi and Aruwimi Rivers. The middle Congo marks the boundary between the

Democratic Republic of the Congo and the Republic of the Congo. Most of the middle Congo, which is about 1,000 miles (1,600 km) long, is navigable. The lower Congo is 270 miles (435 km) long and contains many rapids. Small boats can travel along this section of the river, though large riverboats are unable.

The country also has several large lakes on the eastern border with Uganda, including Lakes Albert, Edward, Kivu, and Tanganyika. All of these lakes sit within the western rift of the Great Rift Valley, a massive geological feature that stretches from the country of Syria in the Middle East to Mozambique in southeastern Africa. The western rift also has two large mountain ranges: the Ruwenzori and the Virunga. The Ruwenzori contains Mount Ngaliema (known to the Western world as Mount Stanley), which reaches 16,765 feet (5,110 meters) above sea level and is the highest point in country. Within the same range is Mount Alexandra, which reaches a height of 16,750 feet (5,105 meters). The Virunga Mountains have several active volcanoes that occasionally threaten this otherwise-peaceful natural setting.

Plant and Animal Life

The tropical forest in northern Congo covers about one-half of the available land in the country. Plants and flowers blossom in the tropical climate, and some grow up to 15 feet (4.5 meters) high. Many different kinds of hardwood, including mahogany and ebony, are logged and harvested for sale. Other trees that are harvested are rubber trees, banana trees, and coconut palms. Mushrooms and other plants are used for making natural medicines.

Reptiles, including lizards and snakes such as cobras, pythons, and vipers, are plentiful in the Congo forests. Whales and dolphins sometimes

Continuing the legacy of gorilla researcher and advocate Dian Fossey, Liz Pearson looks after two orphan gorillas before reintroducing them to their habitat in the rain forest.

appear in the coastal waters. Hippopotamus, crocodiles, and birds live near the rivers and lakes, while antelope, leopards, lions, rhinoceros, and zebra roam the land.

The Great Rift Valley is home to the mountain gorilla and the *bonobo*, a kind of pygmy chimpanzee that only lives in a national park of Congo in the Virunga Mountains. Some scientists believe that bonobos are more like humans than any other animal. They demonstrate human-like traits through high levels of communication and the ability to socialize in groups. Another ape species, the mountain gorilla, roams free in the Virunga Mountains. American zoologist Dian Fossey studied these gorillas in their natural habitat from 1967 to 1985, and through her advocacy for their protection, helped save them from possible extinction.

Since gaining independence, the Congo has been continuously plagued by political unrest, rebel fighting, and ethnic clashes. (Opposite) In the northeastern city of Bunia, a woman carrying a baby passes by a United Nations peacekeeper, 2003. (Right) A jeep rides through a war-torn street in Bukavu, 1967.

2 A Proud and Bloody History

THE DEMOCRATIC REPUBLIC of the Congo has yet to experience a truly democratic form of government. Over the centuries, the peoples of the Congo have suffered through a series of dishonest leaders. These leaders—both native and foreign—have often used the country's vast natural resources for their own gain. Even today, many clashes between Congolese ethnic groups stem largely from greed and competition for resources. This was not always the case, however. The earliest tribes that lived in the Congo were generally peaceful people who had a deep respect for the land and its riches.

The Lost Paradise of the Pygmies

Toward the end of the early prehistorical era known as the Stone Age, the Congo became home to the Pygmies. These first known inhabitants, small and short in stature, lived in the southern savanna. The average height for a male Pygmy was four feet, nine inches. Pygmies lived a simple life, hunting and gathering just enough food to survive while they moved from place to place. They honored the land and its wildlife, and until invaders came, they lived peacefully.

The Bantu-speaking peoples of West Africa, who migrated toward the end of the first millennium B.C., were the first to dominate the Pygmies. The Bantu introduced a more *sedentary* way of living based on farming. Other groups followed the Bantu. In the eighth century A.D., peoples from central Sudan and East Africa migrated and introduced crops like cereals and bananas. Eventually, cattle herding was also introduced, along with the use of iron and copper tools.

During the successive waves of migration, the Pygmies gradually became more isolated as they were forced deeper into the rain forest. Today, only a few Pygmy groups remain in the Ituri forest of the north, and they live off the land as they always have.

Kings and Kingdoms

By the late 14th century, there were several African groups living in the Congo, and it was around this time that the Kongo Kingdom was established. The Luba Empire, which reigned in the late 15th century, was among the most powerful in the Kongo's history. It organized farming villages and established kings as rulers of various states. These kings, believed to have supernatural powers, were feared and respected. Another very powerful group were the Lunda, who from the early 16th century were a dominant force in the southwestern region of the Congo.

Europeans first made contact with natives in 1482, the year that Portuguese explorer Diogo Cão journeyed down the Congo River. Once the Europeans arrived, the vast mineral riches of the region such as copper and diamonds could no longer remain a well-kept secret. A trade relationship with Portugal developed in the 16th century. Over the course of trading, Kongo kings formed bonds with Portuguese leaders of the Catholic Church. Kings and their subjects embraced the Catholic religion, and many Kongo men became Catholic priests. But relations with Portugal first became strained around the time that the Portuguese began trading slaves with the Kongo. Slave trading continued for more than 300 years in this part of Africa.

Another explorer, British-American journalist Henry M. Stanley, led an expedition through the Kongo between 1874 and 1877. Stanley set out in hopes of sparking British interest in the region. He became the first European to navigate the Congo River from source to sea, and through his travels he opened up the once-secret region to outsiders.

A Congolese man stands before a looming statue of the British-American explorer Henry Morton Stanley, who in the 1870s and 1880s led several expeditions into the Congo for Belgium. This photo was taken shortly before President Mobutu Sese Seko ordered that the statues of Stanley and other Western figures be taken down.

The individual who benefited the most from Stanley's explorations was King Leopold II of Belgium. In 1878, Leopold asked Stanley to draw up treaties with local Kongo chiefs and claim land in Leopold's name. Over the next few years, Stanley negotiated 450 treaties, and in 1885, the king announced that the region was now the Congo Free State and he was its ruler.

The people of the Congo were, unfortunately, far from free. For the next 20 years, King Leopold used slave labor to harvest rubber and ivory for *export* to other countries. He kept all profits for himself, and up to one million Congolese slaves are believed to have died from starvation and mistreatment under his rule. Despite the personal wealth he gained, Leopold did not have the resources to further develop the Congo. What was more, he faced heavy criticism from missionaries and influential public figures like American writer Mark Twain, who wrote a famous satire documenting the king's cruel methods in 1905. Eventually, the Belgian government recognized the need to take control of the Congo from the king. In 1908, the colony was renamed again, this time the Belgian Congo.

A Rocky Road to Independence

After the Belgian government took over control of the colony from the king, living conditions improved, and education and medical care were made available to the Congolese people. Nonetheless, the Belgian government still controlled the country's supplies of diamonds, gold, copper, rubber, and palm oil. When Belgium entered World War II in 1940, these natural resources provided much-needed raw material to fund the war.

By the 1950s, the people of the Congo began to protest against Belgian rule. Two of the strongest voices for independence were those of Patrice Lumumba and Joseph Kasavubu, leaders of the ***nationalist*** movement. These men represented conflicting approaches to nationalism. Lumumba, leader of the Congolese National Movement, believed that a strong central government was important to achieve this goal; Kasavubu, head of the cultural association known as Abako, favored sharing powers between the central government and local regions. In 1956, Abako issued a manifesto in response to Professor Antoine van Bilsen's *Thirty-Year Plan for the Political Emancipation of Belgian Africa*, published a year earlier. Rather than accepting the Belgian intellectual's plan for a gradual transfer of power, Abako believed self-government should be granted immediately to the Congolese.

Abako's victories in the 1957 communal council elections in Léopoldville (the capital city, now called Kinshasa) offered further proof that the nationalist movement was gaining steam. When political riots erupted in the capital in 1959, resulting in the deaths of 49 Congolese and the massive looting of European

The first prime minister of the Congo, Patrice Lumumba, speaks at a rally celebrating the country's newly won independence in 1960.

property, the colonial authorities acknowledged that they were losing control. Independence was granted on June 30, 1960, and the country was named the Congo.

A new government was created and in the country's first national elections, Lumumba was named the prime minister and Kasavubu the president. The Belgians still held onto a large share of the power by controlling the army. But in July 1960, just one month after the country gained independence, soldiers in the Congolese army mutinied against their Belgian superiors. The mutiny helped spark uprisings that same month in other parts of the Congo. Two of the country's wealthiest regions, the copper-producing Katanga Province, and the southeastern part of the diamond-rich Kasai Province, made declarations to *secede*. Belgium sent in troops to restore order, a decision that angered many Congolese who felt Belgians were attempting to regain control of the country.

The crisis also fueled disagreements between President Kasavubu and Prime Minister Lumumba. Kasavubu supported Lumumba's appeal to the United Nations to keep the peace, but he strongly disagreed with using U.N. troops to crush the Katanga and Kasai rebellions. Even more divisive was Lumumba's decision to accept assistance from the Soviet Union to quell the resistance. During this period, *Cold War* opposition between the United States and the Soviet Union led to the formation of rival alliances in various regions, including Africa. Lumumba's Soviet ties concerned the United States, Belgium, and other Western powers. They responded by offering more support to Kasavubu over the next few years, which further intensified the power struggle between the two leaders.

Rival ethnic groups fought for control of the Congo, and the central government fell into turmoil as Kasavubu and Lumumba continued to clash over government policy and their leadership roles. In September 1960, Kasavubu dismissed Lumumba and named Joseph Ileo as the new prime minister. Lumumba was put into prison, where he was killed in 1961.

In an attempt to reunify the country, the government met with representatives from all the Congolese provinces in 1961. The leaders of the Kasai Province agreed to rejoin the Congo, but the Katanga Province still held out for independence for two and a half more years. Rebel troops resumed fighting with U.N. forces in December 1962. Finally, a month after the fighting, Katanga admitted defeat and signed an agreement ending the secession.

Weakened by years of conflict, the central government of Congo had yet to establish its authority and was still vulnerable to insurgencies. In March 1965, General Joseph-Désiré Mobutu led the army in a successful military *coup* and named himself president.

Mobutu's Iron Rule

Within a year of assuming the presidency, Mobutu had put into motion his ideas of how the Congolese government should operate. He called himself president, though he acted more like a *dictator*. Seeking to weaken the influence of the Catholic Church on the people, he banned religious instruction in schools and called an end to the official celebration of Christmas. He also changed the names of all the regions (formerly called provinces), replacing the colonial or Christian names with African ones. The biggest change was to the country's name, which became Zaire. For himself, Mobutu later took the

The 32-year dictatorship of Mobutu Sese Seko, which began in 1965, was marred by mismanagement, corruption, and religious persecution. His presidency finally ended when Laurent-Desiree Kabila forcibly removed him in 1997.

name of Mobutu Sese Seko (in his native language, Lingala, this name means "the all-powerful warrior, who because of his endurance and inflexible will to win, will go from conquest to conquest, leaving fire in his wake").

To maintain a firm grip on his power, Mobutu forced out all political parties except his own in 1970, which paved the way for him to win the election that year and begin a seven-year term. In addition to controlling the political system, he aimed to control the national economy, taking over many of the businesses and letting friends and supporters run them. According to Mobutu, the goal was to make Zaire more economically independent, but the plan backfired and the economy collapsed. While the country suffered, the president still quickly became one of the wealthiest individuals in the world, accumulating a personal stash estimated between $6 billion and $10 billion.

Mobutu used the country's natural resources to develop new enterprises. He failed, however, because he focused too much on the mining industry and neglected the agricultural output so crucial to the economy. When copper prices fell in the 1970s, many Zaireans lost their mining jobs. A large segment of the workers had previously been farmers, but had to neglect their crops while working in the mines. With no jobs and no crops, many Congolese farmers died of starvation. To make matters worse, farmers who found modest success often had their crops stolen.

During the late 1970s and throughout the 1980s, the people of Zaire became more desperate, and opposition movements grew stronger. Mobutu realized that he was losing his influence. In 1990 he agreed to end the ban on political parties and appoint a transitional government. The following year he made further concessions after soldiers and civilians staged riots. The people elected a new prime minister and legislature in 1992, after which Mobutu went back on his word and refused to turn over any real power to the new government.

The Fighting Continues

Since 1994, fighting among rebel groups has taken place in the Congo, with each group seeking to expand its power. Some of the combat has involved forces from neighboring Rwanda, where over several decades clashes between ethnic Hutu and Tutsi groups have claimed millions of lives. Rwanda's 1994 civil war resulted in the genocide of an estimated 800,000 Tutsi and moderate Hutu. After the war many Hutu rebels involved in the genocide escaped to Zaire, where they set up military bases from which to carry out attacks against Rwanda's Tutsi-dominated army.

A separate group of Congolese rebels planned to overthrow Mobutu. Supported by Rwanda, Zambia, Angola, and Uganda, these rebels began capturing much of eastern Zaire in 1996, and by May of the following year had taken the city of Kinshasa. Rebel leader Laurent-Desiree Kabila and his troops deposed

President Mobutu and then renamed the country the Democratic Republic of the Congo. Mobutu fled into exile in Morocco, where he died in 1997.

Shortly after setting up the new government, Kabila faced imminent attack from Congolese Tutsi rebels, disturbed by reports that the president's forces had murdered thousands of Rwandan Tutsi refugees. By late 1998, Kabila was fending off the same Rwandan troops that had helped put him into power. Several rebel groups were stationed in northeastern Congo, and from the bases there they launched attacks on the government. Rwanda, Uganda, and Burundi backed the rebels, while neighboring countries Zimbabwe, Angola, and Namibia sent troops to aid Kabila's army. There was a temporary resolution to the conflict in 1999, when the rebel forces, Kabila's government, and the governments of the five other regional countries signed the Lusaka peace agreement. However, both sides continued fighting afterwards, with some of the worst attacks aimed at civilians, especially Tutsis.

A New Presidency

On January 16, 2001, President Laurent Kabila was assassinated, purportedly by one of his bodyguards. His 29-year-old son, Joseph Kabila, was named president 10 days later.

Though young and inexperienced, Joseph Kabila showed potential to be a strong leader. His administration worked with the Rwandan government to end the fighting between the Hutu extremists and Rwandan-backed rebels in the Congo. In July 2002, Rwanda agreed to withdraw the 20,000 troops that were still in the country. In return, the Congo promised it would help find and disarm Hutu rebels who had taken part in the 1994 massacres. In 2003, Joseph

Kabila also negotiated a deal with Uganda to rid the Congo of approximately 6,000 Ugandan troops still in the northeastern region of Ituri. However, rioting broke out between two local ethnic groups, the Hema and the Lendu, which slowed the withdrawal of the troops. Between 2002 and 2003, more than 5,000 people died in fighting in the city of Bunia.

In July 2003, Joseph Kabila signed a constitution that established yet another new government. The leaders agreed that power would be shared by the different ethnic groups, including the main rebel parties. This *interim government* would remain until new presidential elections are held and a permanent constitution is created. The elections were scheduled to take place in 2005, but by April of that year it seemed likely they would be delayed.

The promise of peace and true democracy for the Congo has yet to be fulfilled. More than 3 million citizens have died in the country's civil wars, and many more have had their crops burned or stolen, or have had to flee their homes. But with a new government pledging to restore stability, there is hope once again that freedom and democracy is within reach.

The overthrow of President Mobutu in 1997 was met with jubilation by Zaireans, as they were called during the years of the president's rule. These men celebrate by smashing government weapons in Kinshasa.

(Opposite) President Joseph Kabila and U.S. president George W. Bush meet at the White House, 2003. Bush and other Western leaders supported a new Congolese constitution that included a power-sharing agreement. (Right) A supporter of one of the rebel leaders, Jean-Pierre Bemba, holds up a pennant; its translation reads, "With God we shall overcome."

3 Turmoil and Transition

THE CONGOLESE HAVE passed through several constitutions and governments since the country gained its freedom from Belgium in 1960. The most recent government, led by President Joseph Kabila, was made official with a new constitution in April 2003. This interim government is moving toward democracy, as illustrated by its even distribution of power among the executive, legislative, and judicial branches.

The main divisions of the interim government of the Congo are the president, the courts, and the Parliament, which is comprised of the National Assembly and the Senate. For the sake of preserving the peace among the various Congolese factions, President Kabila shares power with four new vice presidents, all former rebel leaders. They are Jean-Pierre Bemba, Arthur Zahidi Ngoma, Azarias Ruberwa, and Abdoulaye Yerodia Ndombasi. Kabila and his vice presidents hold regular discussions over how the permanent government will operate. They have agreed that presidential elections will be held every seven years, the next one scheduled for 2005. All Congolese citizens over the age of 18 will be required to vote in this election.

Powers of the Executive Branch

The president has the authority to establish laws, which is done through an official order, or *decree*. However, before proceeding he or she must consult the ministers and vice presidents. The president is also commander of the armed forces and appoints several officials, including *ambassadors*, provincial governors, members of the Supreme Court, army and police officers, and the head of the central bank. He or she has the authority to pardon crimes and declare war, following an official recommendation and approval by the National Assembly and Senate.

Each vice president is responsible for one of four important government functions: security and defense, economics and finance, reconstruction and development, and social and cultural activity. Each leader supervises a group of ministers who carry out the responsibilities related to these fields.

There are 35 officials who make up the *cabinet* of ministers. They advise the president and vice presidents on issues such as national defense, foreign affairs, and citizens' health and welfare. They are also responsible for seeing that the decisions and plans made by the president and vice presidents are carried out.

Cabinet ministers serve on special committees, one of which is a powerful advisory group known as the National Defense Council. Members of

(Left to right) Vice Presidents Arthur Zahidi Ngoma, Jean-Pierre Bemba, Azarias Ruberwa, and Abdoulaye Yerodia Ndombasi attend an inauguration ceremony in July 2003. As leaders of the interim government formed that year, these former rebel leaders play a critical role in establishing a lasting peace.

this council include the president, the four vice presidents, the minister of defense, the minister of home affairs, the decentralization and security minister, and the chiefs of staff of the armed forces. The president consults the council on the formation and structure of the armed forces, the disarmament and withdrawal of foreign troops, and other matters of national defense. Before declaring a war, he or she must always consult the National Defense Council.

Parliament

The Parliament contains two bodies—the Senate and the National Assembly. Together they discuss, review, and vote on the bills sent to them by the president. The Senate has 120 members who were appointed by the interim government shortly after it was formed. They represent the 11 administrative areas of the country—the 10 provinces and the city of Kinshasa—and are responsible for creating the new permanent constitution. The National Assembly has 500 members, called deputies, who were also appointed by the interim government.

It takes a majority of both the Senate and the National Assembly to pass a bill. If they disagree over legislation, a Joint Consultative Committee is established to try to reach an agreement. If the problem is not resolved, the National Assembly makes the final ruling. Once a bill is passed, it is sent back to the president, who within 15 days makes an official decree that it is law. If there is a question about whether the bill is in conformance with the interim constitution, the president may send it to the Supreme Court to decide on the matter.

Supreme Court and Lower Courts

The court system of the Congo is based on a mix of tribal and Belgian civil law. Each administrative division has its own court, presided over by judges with the titles of governor and deputy governor. Lower courts oversee local disagreements, and each division has appeals courts, which hear cases that have been challenged. The Supreme Court acts independently and rules on any disputes that arise between the executive and legislative branches.

Although the civil system is well established, many Congolese still prefer to use tribal law to settle disputes. When a disagreement arises among two individuals or groups, a local chief will often hear from the parties and issue a ruling. The courts honor the decisions of the tribal courts as long as they do not upset the peace.

Despite its great mineral wealth, the Congo's economy labors to meet the needs of the people after struggling through years of war. (Opposite) A worker sprays solution on copper sheets at a plant in Katanga Province, where there are extensive reserves of copper. (Right) Refugees of ethnic conflict are provided food at a hospital.

4 The Costs of War

EVEN THOUGH THE Congo is rich in natural resources, most of its people live in poverty. The current situation is largely the result of five years of war, which has allowed for government corruption, the looting of natural resources, and the deterioration of the infrastructure.

Nearly every Congolese citizen has firsthand experience of the country's weak economy. A study by the World Health Organization in 2001 reported that the average Congolese lives on about 20 cents a day, and consumes less than two-thirds of the calories needed to maintain basic health. AIDS and other diseases spread rapidly, as people generally do not have enough money to buy the necessary medicines.

Mining

Mining has always been extremely important to the Congo's economy, responsible for approximately 11 percent of its **gross domestic product (GDP)**. In 1999, diamond exports brought in more than 61 percent of the country's export revenue. Copper and cobalt are other leading exports. It is uncertain just how many of the approximately 22 million people of the Congo's labor force are miners, because this industry contains many illegal workers, including foreign troops.

Most Congolese miners live in the southern province of Katanga, the center of the country's mining industry. Katanga mines contain much of the world's cobalt and large supplies of copper, and are also rich in gold, zinc, uranium, manganese, tin ore, coal, and silver. Coltan, a mineral used in the manufacture of cell phones and other electronic devices, is mined in the Ituri Forest and in other areas of the eastern Congo. It is estimated that 80 percent of the world's reserves of coltan are in the Congo. The country's diamonds are mostly mined in Kasai.

Although the Congo's mines have great potential, war, political instability, and corruption have taken a toll on the copper industry. At state-run mining companies, production has fallen sharply over the past decade. One state-run company that used to produce around 450,000 tons of copper per year only produced about 30,000 tons in 2001.

The production of coltan has also decreased in recent years. Early in 2001, a kilogram of coltan was worth around $80; by the end of that year, the price had fallen to about $8 per kilogram. Although the price decline was in part due to competition from a new Australian mining company, corruption was also a factor, as the United States and other leading importers had stopped importing coltan upon discovering it was being illegally traded. In 2001, coltan had also taken the place of diamonds as the country's leading illegal export.

The High Cost of War

Civil war and corruption have cost the Congolese dearly. From the late 1990s until 2003, foreign troops from Uganda, Zimbabwe, and Angola took part in illegal mining in the midst of the wars. A few corrupt leaders benefited from the bribes offered by foreign troops while export prices continued to fall, causing mines to close and many Congolese to lose their jobs. A report by the International Monetary Fund said that in 2001, as much as one-third of the estimated $300 million of total diamond production was illegally smuggled out of the Congo by foreign troops.

As president, Joseph Kabila has worked hard to revive the Congo's economy, beginning with reopening some of the country's plentiful mines. In 2001, 20,988 tons of copper, 12 million carats of industrial diamonds, and 6.2 million carats of gem-quality diamonds were mined. Currently, the Congo has an estimated 75 million tons of copper, 1 billion tons of iron ore, 240 million carats of diamonds, and 600 tons of gold waiting to be mined.

Forestry and Agriculture

About 75 percent of the Congo is covered in trees, and 45 percent of the land area is equatorial rain forest. Thus, forestry and logging are important industries in which teak, ebony, and other woods are logged and sold.

A Congolese woman sells fruit in the main street of Bunia. Food crops like bananas, oranges, and mangoes are grown for sale in the Congo and are also sold abroad.

Although much of the land in the Congo is not available for farming, agriculture still makes up 65 percent of the country's labor force, and farming was responsible for 56 percent of the country's gross domestic product in 2001. Most farmers grow just enough food to support themselves. However, some foods are grown for sale within the country and for export to other countries. Food crops include bananas, mangoes, and oranges as well as corn, beans, rice, cassava, and peanuts. Rubber, palm oil, cotton, coffee, tea, and sugar cane are generally grown for export. All kinds of livestock—goats, sheep, cattle, pigs, and chickens—are raised in the Congo, and more than 200,000 tons of fish are caught each year.

The Congo spent an estimated $890 million on *imports* in 2002. Major imports include food, machinery, and fuel, much of which comes from Belgium, South Africa, France, Germany, Italy, and the United States. Most of the imports to the Congo come from South Africa and Belgium.

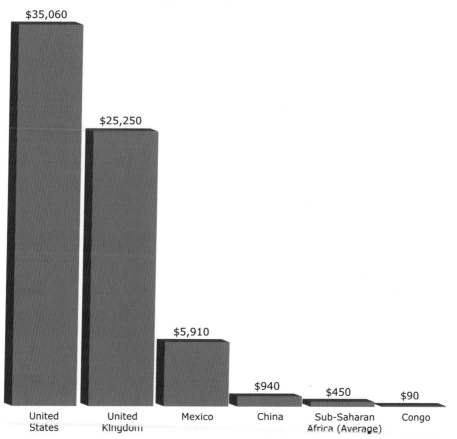

Gross National Income (GNI) Per Capita of the Congo and Other Countries*

$35,060 — United States
$25,250 — United Kingdom
$5,910 — Mexico
$940 — China
$450 — Sub-Saharan Africa (Average)
$90 — Congo

*Gross national income per capita is the total value of all goods and services produced domestically in a year, supplemented by income received from abroad, divided by midyear population. The above figures take into account fluctuations in currency exchange rates and differences in inflation rates across global economies.

Figures are 2002 estimates. Source: World Bank, 2003.

Exports, which primarily include copper, diamonds, cobalt, and oil, reached a total of $1.2 billion in 2002. Belgium is the Congo's main export partner, though it also sells goods to the United States, Zimbabwe, and Finland.

Transportation and Energy

The Congo desperately needs improvements to its road and rail system. Because it is so difficult to bring goods to market in the Congo, the country's trading power is seriously limited. Though 93,200 miles (150,000 km) of road exists, only about 20,500 miles (33,000 km) of it is paved, and during the rainy season many roads are impassable. War damages have also debilitated much of the rail lines, which total 3,193 miles (5,138 km) in length.

Traders seeking an alternative to the country's inefficient road system use river transport. Regular riverboat traffic runs between Kinshasa and Kisangani and between Kinshasa and Ilebo on the Lualaba River. From Kinshasa, the country's major ocean shipping port, goods are transported over Lake Tanganyika and then sent by rail to the seaport of Dar es Salaam in Tanzania.

On the Congo River, riverboats carry as many as 3,000 people. During boat trips, passengers often pass the time by trading. Imported goods, such as cigarettes, clothing, and batteries, are exchanged for local goods like coffee, timber, and palm oil. The civil war in the Congo made travel unsafe for five years, and during that time the number of riverboat trips between Kinshasa and Kisangani dipped dramatically. But peace talks held in 2003 have restored confidence and business on the river has picked up.

Passengers crowd into an early commuter train in Kinshasa. With the infrastructure in desperate need of improvement, most Congolese rely on planes and riverboats for traveling, though in times of war even these forms of transport have been unsafe.

Quick Facts: The Economy of the Democratic Republic of the Congo

Gross domestic product (GDP*): $34 billion

Inflation: 16% (2003 est.)

Natural Resources: cobalt, copper, cadmium, petroleum, industrial and gem diamonds, gold, silver, zinc, manganese, tin, germanium, uranium, radium, bauxite, iron ore, coal, hydropower, timber

Agriculture (55% of GDP): coffee, sugar, palm oil, rubber, tea, quinine, cassava (tapioca), palm oil, bananas, root crops, corn, fruits; wood products (2000 est.)

Industry (11% of GDP): mining (diamonds, copper, zinc), mineral processing, consumer products (including textiles, footwear, cigarettes, processed foods and beverages), cement (2000 est.)

Services (34% of GDP): government, other (2000 est.)

Economic Growth Rate: 3.5%

Foreign Trade:

Exports–$1.2 billion: diamonds, copper, crude oil, coffee, cobalt

Imports–$890 million: foodstuffs, mining, and other machinery, transport equipment, fuels

Currency Exchange Rate: U.S. $1 = 550 Congolese francs (2004)

*GDP, or gross domestic product, is the total value of goods and services produced in a country annually.
All figures are 2002 estimates unless otherwise indicated.
Sources: CIA World Factbook, 2003; Bloomberg.com.

The Congo River contains a greater volume of water than any other river except the Amazon, and also has numerous rapids and waterfalls. Thus, the country has the potential to create huge amounts of *hydroelectricity*. Currently, 97 percent of the electricity used in the Congo comes from hydroelectric sources, but due to the lack of power plants, much of the power still goes untapped.

Hope for a Brighter Future

In January 2002, President Joseph Kabila requested international financial assistance as the country continued making advances toward restoring peace. Many countries provided funds, and the World Bank offered emergency aid to help revitalize agriculture and other economic sectors. Later that year, the reduction of rebel armies promised to further stabilize the marketplace. The rate of inflation, which was as high as 544 percent in 2000, finally fell and hovered around 16 percent in 2002. Export increases in recent years also indicate the national economy is improving. In 2003, the Congo's exports of electricity to Zimbabwe and South Africa more than doubled, and a mutual trade agreement with South Africa in March 2004 signaled further growth.

(Opposite) Sitting second from left is Kasonge Niembo, chief of the Luba people. Although the chiefs of the Luba and the other tribes do not have the same stature as they used to, they are still revered. (Right) The typical community in the Congo remains a village comprised of homes made from mud, sticks, and other natural materials.

5 Language, Identity, and Culture

THE EARLIEST KNOWN ancestors of the Congolese, the Pygmies, were a small and short-statured people who settled in the forests. Toward the end of the first millennium B.C., the taller and darker-skinned Bantu-speaking people moved into the Congo basin from present-day Nigeria and Cameroon. The Nilotic peoples of Sudan soon arrived as well, though throughout the precolonial era the Bantu remained the largest group in the region. Today, the country is home to more than 200 different groups, of which the Luba, Kongo, Lunda, and Mongo make up the largest population segment.

Main Ethnic Groups

Luba people live mostly in the southern provinces of the Congo, in Katanga and Kasai. Luba chiefs, sometimes called kings, were very powerful during the 1400s. They ruled over a large number of villages and tribes, and their influenced spanned a far greater region than that of other chiefs of the Congo.

The Kongo tribe, comprised of people from present-day Angola and the southwestern region of the Congo, was the first group to have contact with the Europeans, who arrived in the late 15th century. Kongo villages gradually came together to form larger groups. Some Kongo chiefs, like the Luba chiefs before them, became very dominant and often took slaves from the tribes of nearby villages.

The Kongo benefited from early contact with the Europeans. They were among the first people of the region to receive schooling, which ultimately gave them more political influence. When the push for Congo's independence began much later in the 1950s, some of the most politically active people were members of the Kongo ethnic group.

The Lunda people live in the southern province of Katanga, between the Lubilash and Kasai Rivers. Some members of the tribe also live in neighboring Angola and Zambia as well. There are a number of smaller tribal groups among the Lunda that are distinguished by their region and modes of lineage. These include the southern Lunda and the Chokwe (or Cokwe), who through their domination of the Lunda in the 19th century have become historically linked with the group. Both of these smaller groups trace their origins through their mother's ancestral lineage. The northern Lunda, also known as the Ruund, trace their origins through both their parents' ancestors. Today, tensions still remain high between the Lunda and the Chokwe.

Quick Facts: The People of the Democratic Republic of the Congo

Population: 56,625,039

Ethnic Groups: over 200 African ethnic groups of which the majority are Bantu; the four largest tribes—Mongo, Luba, Kongo (all Bantu), and the Mangbetu-Azande (Hamitic) make up about 45% of the population

Age structure:
  0–14 years: 48.3%
  15–64 years: 49.2%
  65 years and over: 2.5%

Population growth rate: 2.9%

Birth rate: 45.12 births/1,000 population

Infant mortality rate: 96.56 deaths/1,000 live births

Death rate: 14.87 deaths/1,000 population

Life expectancy at birth:
  total population: 48.93 years
  male: 46.83 years
  female: 51.09 years

Total fertility rate: 6.69 children born/woman

Religion: Roman Catholic 50%, Protestant 20%, Kimbanguist 10%, Muslim 10%, other syncretic sects and indigenous beliefs 10%

Languages: French (official), Lingala (a lingua franca trade language), Kingwana (a dialect of Kiswahili or Swahili), Kikongo, Tshiluba

Literacy: 65.5%

All figures are 2003 estimates unless otherwise indicated.
Source: Adapted from CIA World Factbook, 2003.

The Mongo people live in the Congo River basin and the area to the south extending to the Kasai and San Kuru Rivers. The early Mongo people were comprised of many groups who claimed a common ancestor of that name. The village was traditionally the *autonomous* seat of power for the Mongo; however, since the Congo's independence the Mongo's government has extended beyond the village level.

Most of the Congolese people are from Bantu-speaking groups. Each ethnic group has its own language, which means there are actually about 200 different spoken languages, though most have enough in common with other languages that people of different tribes can converse with each other. Dominant languages that are spoken in the Congo are Kikongo, Lingala, Swahili, and Tshiluba. As the official national language, French is used in the government sector and is sometimes taught in school; however, the Congolese rarely speak French in daily conversation today. Instead, they more commonly speak Swahili or Lingala.

Keeping the Village Ties

The Congolese place great importance on group identity. The *clan* and tribe one belongs to, or the village one comes from, is a source of personal identity and social status. Often families live in the same village, in which case clan and village identity are the same. When a family moves to another village, it may take on the new village's identity.

For the early Congolese, maintaining group identity was a way to gain political or social power within the community. Most villages were governed by local chiefs, some of whom gained more authority than others and ruled more than one village. All chiefs came into power through their ancestral lines.

When Belgium took over the Congo, hundreds of villages were combined into a manageable number of regions to more easily govern them. Thereafter, village ties became less important, though many Congolese still remained loyal to their immediate neighbors. Even today, it is often expected for Congolese to help others in need if they come from the same village.

Rural Life and Architecture

Most Congolese live in small rural villages, deep in the forest or along the banks of the country's rivers and lakes. These communities may be home to as few as 20 to 30 people or as many as several hundred people. Here people travel by boat—either ferry boat or dugout canoe. Most villagers farm the land to survive, eating most of the food they grow.

A typical Congolese diet often includes a stew made from cornmeal or cassava flour. Fruits such as pineapples and *plantains* are also common, but rural Congolese also eat whatever is available to them from their forest home. They will eat antelope, field rats, birds, and some snakes, even extremely poisonous ones such as vipers. Since the Congo is literally crawling with dangerous snakes and other wild animals, children are taught about them at an early age. They learn not only how to live safely among dangerous creatures, but also how to use them for food.

Insects such as grasshoppers, termites, palm grubs (beetle larvae), and crickets are also part of the Congolese diet. To harvest palm grubs, farmers first cut a hole in the palm tree, attracting female beetles to lay their eggs there. When the eggs hatch, the beetles begin to eat the palm leaves, then the farmers harvest the grubs. Before they are eaten, the insects are fried with salt and hot peppers.

The houses of rural Congolese villagers are typically made from mud, sticks, and other natural materials. Frameworks consist of sticks and palm stems, which are held together by ropes and vines found in nearby marshes. Roofs are made from grass and vines. A mix of sandy soil and water is packed between the sticks to form the walls. Sometimes a little concrete is added to the mix to make it stronger.

If a family is well off, it may be able to afford a tin roof. Along with protecting the home, the tin roof also helps collect rainwater, which is an alternative source of drinking water in places where fresh water is not readily available. From the roof the rain is caught in pans or bowls. This water is often safer than water from the Congo's lakes and streams, many of which are polluted.

Education

All Congolese children aged 6 to 12 are required by law to attend school, though in the rural regions, where schools and resources are sparse, attendance is not widely enforced. Additional schooling is optional beyond age 12. If students choose to go further, they go through what are called educational cycles. The first cycle is two years long, and the second one lasts four more years.

Before the Congo gained independence, instruction beyond the primary grades was limited. Education was only obtained in larger cities, and it was for the purpose of training people for government jobs. Since independence, educational opportunities have increased in the cities, but they remain limited in rural areas. Between 1977 and 2003, the national dropout rate for children rose from 49 percent to 75 percent. In 2000, about 42 percent of the population had never been to school; another 42 percent had gained a primary education; 15 percent had a secondary education; and only 1 percent of the population had acquired a college degree.

A representative from an AIDS support group educates Kinshasa school-children about the dangers of AIDS. Education is pivotal in the fight against the pandemic, though with the Congo's school dropout rate at 75 percent in 2003, many children are not present at schools to learn about AIDS.

The Arts

Congolese artists are well known for their decorative masks. Traditional masks made of leather, wood, metal, or fabric have been used for thousands of years in *rituals* and celebrations. People wear masks for celebrations of crop harvests or rites of passage, such as when a child comes of age and officially

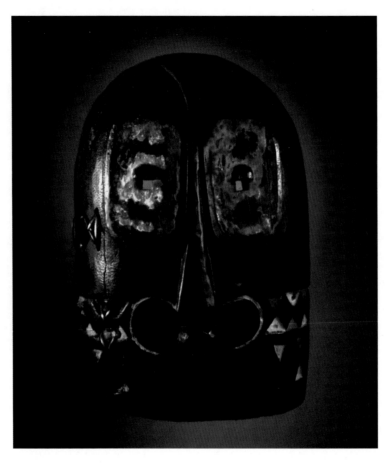

A mask made by a member of the Bembe, a Bantu people living in southeastern Congo. Many ethnic groups of the Congo are known for their decorative masks, which are used in traditional celebrations of crop harvests and rites of passage.

enters the adult community. Masks are decorated to honor the spirits of gods, ancestors, and animals. Sometimes they are made to honor evil spirits in hopes of appeasing them.

Copper and stone are two materials that are commonly found in Congolese art. Copper art is especially popular in Katanga, where large reserves of the mineral are found. The copper is first flattened into a thin sheet. Then an image, often of a person or animal, is pounded into the soft metal. Clay is mixed with other materials to make a colored paste used to paint the image. The piece is then placed over a fire, which brings out the final colors and textures.

Malachite, a colored rock of copper oxide found in Lubumbashi, is often used to make small useful objects such as chess pieces, jewelry boxes, vases, and picture frames. Shapes are cut or ground out of the rock, and then a special machine polishes the finished pieces. Other common Congolese art objects include pottery and colorful textile goods, such as fabrics that feature vivid patterns and colors.

Music has always been a significant part of Congolese life, and is considered a special way to communicate through rhythm. Singing, clapping, and foot stamping often serve as accompaniment. Drums are popular musical instruments, as are bells, rattles, gongs, and flutes. Instruments may be made from *gourds* or clay pots. Congolese music, which is strongly influenced by a kind of Cuban dance music known as rumba, is popular throughout Africa. Since the 1950s, Kinshasa has been a major center where rumba musicians and other enthusiasts of Latin American music congregate and share ideas. In their performances, the Congolese have made the music their own by adding what are known as "animations," verbal instructions given to dancers by the musicians.

Traditional Congolese dances are often a part of special events such as weddings and other celebrations. On these occasions, dancers may paint their bodies and wear costumes with masks and feathers. Wedding celebrations may last for days with feasts for the entire community. They are a rare occasion during which a Congolese woman is given more respect than a man.

A popular diversion for the Congolese is a board game called *ngola*, which is played with dried peas or marbles.

Games and Recreation

Congolese people, like most people everywhere, enjoy playing games. One of the country's most popular games is *ngola*, a board game played with dried peas or marbles. Typically, two people play, though sometimes teams are formed. *Ngola* is similar to chess or checkers—also popular in the Congo—in that the object of the game is to capture the other person's pieces by moving your pieces around the board. Congolese people also play card games and dice games, which may involve gambling.

Soccer, which was introduced by Catholic missionaries in the early 1900s, is one of the country's most popular team sports. Watching soccer games and tournaments is a favorite Congolese pastime. The national team won the coveted African Nations Cup (an international tournament held every two years) in 1968, 1974, and 1994.

Boxing and track and field are other popular Congolese sports. The Congo is still remembered within the boxing community as the country that hosted the "Rumble in the Jungle," the legendary world championship match in 1974 between Muhammad Ali and George Foreman, held in Kinshasa.

Soccer is the national sport of the Congo. These loyal fans of the national team, in attendance at an African Nations Cup match, wear shirts with President Joseph Kabila's image.

The Congo is home to both modern cities and rural villages. (Opposite) The capital city of Kinshasa, which rests on the Congo River and has an international airport, is a trade and transportation hub. (Right) The eastern village of Kanyabayonga is one of countless traditional communities in the country.

6 Cities and Communities

THE CONGO IS divided into 11 administrative divisions, which include 10 provinces and the capital city, Kinshasa. At one time, each province ran its own administration almost independently of the central government. However, since 1967 the federal government has had greater authority over the provinces.

Both city life and rural life can be found in their extremes in the Congo. Modern-looking cities with cars and skyscrapers are just a riverboat ride away from small communities where people live in houses of mud and sticks. Whether they live in cities or rural communities, however, one thing many Congolese have in common is poverty.

Kinshasa

About 6.8 million Congolese, or more than 10 percent of the country's population, were recorded as living in Kinshasa in 2004. It is the Congo's most modern city, the seat of government, and the economic center. Many government offices are located here, including the Supreme Court.

When the city was founded in 1881, British explorer Henry Stanley named it Léopoldville in honor of King Leopold II. Léopoldville replaced Boma as the capital of the Belgian Congo in 1926. Six years after the Congo's independence in 1960, the city was renamed Kinshasa, after an African village located in the area since 1881.

Kinshasa sits directly on the Congo River, and so receives goods traveling from Kisangani, located in the northeast. From Kinshasa, the goods are then transported by railcar to the port of Matadi. The city boasts a large international airport that hosts flights between the Congo and Europe, North America, and South America. The Republic of the Congo, located across the Congo River to the west, is reached by motorboat or riverboat.

Visitors to Kinshasa will likely note the different lifestyles of its rich and poor residents. Along the riverbank in the city's industrial heart, government offices, tall buildings, and stores indicate the wealth of the neighborhood. To the south, farther down the river, some of the country's poorest people live in mud-brick homes without plumbing or electricity.

As the educational and cultural center of the Congo, Kinshasa has 3 universities, 14 teacher-training colleges, and 18 technical schools. Lovanium University, one of the country's major universities, has a research center for

There are four national universities in the Congo: one in Lubumbashi (pictured above), another in Kisangani, and two in Kinshasa. With limited room for enrollment, few students have the opportunity to attend college in the Congo—in 2000, only 1 percent of the population had earned a degree.

the study of tropical medicines, a museum of African culture, and an archae-
ology museum.

More than 60 percent of the people in Kinshasa are *literate*.
Approximately 124,000 people read nine daily newspapers. Residents of
Kinshasa own about 18 million radios and 6.5 million televisions. There is
one educational radio station in the city, as well as radio and television sta-
tions that are controlled by the government.

Katanga Province and Lubumbashi

Katanga, called Shaba under Mobutu's rule, is one of the Congo's
major industrial areas. It is a large province, covering about 200,000 square
miles (518,000 sq km), and is located in south, bordering Angola on the
southwest, Zambia on the southeast, and Lake Tanganyika on the northeast. The lucrative industry of copper mining makes Katanga one of the
Congo's wealthiest provinces, yet it also experiences some of the country's
most violent weather.

Lubumbashi is the capital of Katanga. Located near the border of
Zambia, the city had a population of about 1,140,000 people in 2004, making it the second-largest city in the Congo after Kinshasa. Formerly known
as Elisabethville, Lubumbashi was founded in 1910 by *immigrants* from
Britain, South Africa, Australia, and other countries. The early settlers were
drawn to the surrounding area's thriving copper industry. Copper mining
greatly expanded in Katanga with the arrival of the first railroads in 1910.

Lubumbashi is still rich in mineral resources today. In addition to its
copper, it has large amounts of cobalt, tin, coal, and zinc. It also has a

modern airport and a railroad line running through the city. The University of Kinshasa is located there, as well as a regional museum that boasts a valuable collection of African art.

Other Major Cities

Thanks to its supply of diamonds, the Kasai-Occidental Province is another of the Congo's wealthier provinces. Its capital, Kananga, had an estimated population of 576,000 in 2004. The city is located in south-central Congo on the Lulua River, and was known as Luluabourg during the colonial era.

Founded by German explorer Hermann von Wissmann in 1884, Kananga experienced rapid growth in the early 1900s when the railroads reached the Congo. Today, it is still a center for processing and transporting goods such as cotton and coffee, much of which is farmed on land outside the city. Both the Luba and the Lulua tribes call the city home, though they share a troubled history that dates back to the late 1950s, when land disputes between the tribes erupted in violence.

Kisangani, the capital of Orientale Province, is located in north-central Congo, just north of Boyoma Falls. Founded in 1883 by British explorer Henry Stanley, the city was known as Stanleyville until 1966. As a port city on the Congo River, it receives much of the river traffic of the northeastern region.

Kisangani has an international airport and a railroad line linking it to Ubundi, a city located toward the south along the Congo River. Kisangani is also a center of manufacturing for goods such as metal products and furniture.

In Kisangani, this taxi driver provides his service via bicycle, a common form of transport in this north-central city. Kisangani is a port city on the Congo that harnesses much of the river's hydroelectric energy.

Beer, cotton, and rice are produced for export, and the river is a source of hydroelectricity. An agricultural institute and a satellite campus of the University of Kinshasa are also located in the city.

Matadi, the Congo's main ocean port city, had a population of 235,400 in

2004. It is located in the western province of Bas-Congo, about 80 miles (130 km) from the mouth of the Congo River. Railway lines link Matadi to Kinshasa, and exported goods, mainly coffee and timber, are shipped from there.

Another port city in the Bas-Congo Province is Boma, which between 1887 and 1926 was the capital of the Congo Free State. The city is larger than Matadi with a 2004 population of about 375,500. It also has railway lines, and exports timber, palm products, bananas, and other food products.

A Calendar of Congolese Festivals

January

On January 1, **New Year's Day**, Congolese celebrate with music and dancing.

Congolese observe **Martyrs of Independence Day** on January 4 to honor people who died in the fight for independence.

May

Labour Day, an international day reserved to remember and respect all workers, is held on May 1.

June

On June 30, **Independence Day**, Congolese remember the day of their independence from Belgium with speeches, parades, music, and feasting.

August

August 1 is reserved for **Parents' Day**, a holiday remembering ancestors. Many Congolese go to the family cemetery plot to redecorate graves. They will often hold a meal there before returning home to spend the rest of the day with family.

November

November 1, **All Saints' Day**, is a Catholic religious holiday on which people honor the saints of the early Church.

Armed Forces Day (also called **Army Day**), November 17, is an occasion to show respect for the military, which has played a pivotal role in the lives of Congolese people.

December

On December 25, **Christmas**, Christians celebrate by inviting friends for dinner, which is often served outside in the open air.

Kwanzaa is a celebration that started in Africa and is observed by Congolese and other African peoples. *Kwanzaa* means "first fruits of the harvest" in Swahili. Originally a harvest celebration, today it celebrates African heritage, and goes on for seven days between the 26th and 31st of December. During the celebration, people light candles, one for each day of the week, in a special candleholder. They sometimes dance and give one another gifts that represent their culture. On December 31, the seventh day of Kwanzaa, families celebrate with a special feast called Karamu.

66

A Calendar of Congolese Festivals

Religious Observances

Congolese Christians observe a number of important holy days, as do Congolese Muslims, who make up 10 percent of the population. Some of these are on particular days each year (for example, Christmas is always observed on December 25). However, many other major celebrations are held according to a lunar calendar, in which the months are related to the phases of the moon. A lunar month is shorter than the typical month of the Western calendar. Therefore, the festival dates vary from year to year. Other celebrations are observed seasonally.

A very important month of the Muslim lunar calendar is the ninth month, **Ramadan**. This is a time of sacrifice for devout Muslims. Congolese Muslims celebrate **Eid al Fitr** to mark the end of Ramadan. **Eid al-Adha** (Feast of Sacrifice) takes place in the last month of the Muslim calendar during the hajj period, when Muslims make a pilgrimage to Mecca. The holiday honors the prophet Abraham, who was willing to sacrifice his own son to Allah. Each of these holidays is celebrated with a feast. On Eid al-Adha, families traditionally eat a third of the feast and donate the rest to the poor.

The major Christian festivals on the lunar cycle involve the suffering and death of Jesus Christ. **Ash Wednesday** marks the start of a period of self-sacrifice called **Lent**, which lasts for 40 days. The final eight days of Lent are known as **Holy Week**. A number of important days are observed, including **Palm Sunday**, which commemorates Jesus' arrival in Jerusalem; **Holy Thursday**, which marks the night of the Last Supper; **Good Friday**, the day of Jesus' death on the cross; and **Easter Monday**, which marks his resurrection. (In Western countries, Easter is typically celebrated on the day before.) On **Ascension Day**, 40 days after Easter, people celebrate the rising of Jesus from earth to heaven.

67

Recipes

Peanut Sauce

2 spoonfuls of oil
1/2 small onion, finely minced
1 cup roasted, shelled, skinned, and mashed
   peanuts (or 1 cup peanut butter)
2 cups water (or chicken broth/stock)
Salt, cayenne pepper or red pepper (to taste)
1 fresh hot chili pepper, finely minced (optional)

Directions:
1. Heat oil in skillet. Fry onions and optional fresh pepper in oil, until soft, and set aside.
2. Combine peanuts (or peanut butter), water, salt, and spices in sauce pan. Stir until smooth and simmer over low heat for 10 to 15 minutes.
3. Add onions and hot pepper. Stir and simmer until completely heated.
4. Serve over grilled chicken, meat, or fish, or with rice. It can also be served as a soup.

Kelewele (Spicy Fried Plantains)

4 to 6 plantain bananas, slightly under-ripe or ripe, but not past ripe, peeled, and cut into bite-sized cubes
1/2 tsp. cayenne pepper or red pepper
1/2 tsp. peeled, grated fresh ginger root
1 tsp. salt
2 Tbsp. water
Palm oil or vegetable oil for frying

Directions:
1. Grind together grated ginger root, pepper, and salt; then mix with water.
2. In a glass bowl, toss together the plantain cubes and spice mixture.
3. In a deep skillet, heat oil (just deep enough to allow plantains to float) to 350°F. Fry plantains, turning once, until golden brown on both sides. (Don't try to fry them all at once; they should not touch each other while frying.)
4. Drain on absorbent paper; keep in warmed oven until all the plantains are fried. Serve *kelewele* immediately.

Chicken in Peanut-Tomato Sauce

Peanut oil (or any cooking oil)
1 chicken (for the gourmet version, 4 to 6 chicken breasts), cut into bite-sized or serving-sized pieces
1–2 onions, cut up
1–2 cloves of garlic, minced (optional)
1 cup tomato paste (or tomato sauce)
1 cup peanut butter (natural or homemade is best)
1 cup water
Cayenne pepper or red pepper, black pepper, salt

Directions:

1. Heat a couple spoonfuls of oil in a deep pot. Add the chicken and fry it on both sides until it is browned and nearly done. Remove the chicken and set aside. (Note: It might be best to fry part of the chicken and remove it, and then repeat the process two or three times. Chicken cooks best if the chicken pieces do not touch each other while frying.)
2. Fry the onions and garlic in the same pot. Stir in tomato paste. Reduce heat and simmer for a few minutes.
3. Return chicken to pot. Stir in peanut butter (if using peanuts, first shell and roast them, then grind or mash them into a paste, adding water if needed). Be sure to use a very low heat or peanut butter will scorch.
4. Stir in enough water to make tomato paste and peanut butter into a smooth sauce. Add spices to taste. Stir. Simmer on low heat until chicken is done.
5. Serve with fried or boiled plantains or rice.

Oven or grill variation: Use larger chicken pieces. Follow all directions but without chicken. Cook sauce over low heat until heated through. (Use low heat; be careful not to scorch.) Cook chicken in oven or on an outdoor grill. Pour sauce on chicken after chicken is done.

Moambé Stew

2–3 lbs. stew meat, cut into large bite-sized pieces
Juice of a lemon, or juice of one-half of a grapefruit
Salt to taste
Minced chili pepper, or ground cayenne pepper or red pepper (to taste)
2 Tbsp. palm oil, or peanut oil or vegetable oil
2 onions, chopped
6–8 ripe tomatoes, chopped (or canned tomatoes)
Greens (such as spinach, collards, kale, or similar), washed and cut into pieces (optional)
1 cup peanut butter

Directions:

1. Mix together the meat, juice, salt, and hot pepper. Allow to marinate for a half-hour or more.
2. Heat the oil in a dutch oven or large pot. Add the onions, and cook for a few minutes. Add the meat and cook until it is browned.
3. Add the tomatoes and a few cups of water. Reduce heat.
4. Add the peanut butter and the greens (if desired). Cover and simmer on low heat until meat is tender, about an hour.
5. Serve with rice.

All recipes are taken from *The Congo Cookbook*, www.congo-cookbook.com; © 1999–2003 Ed Gibbon, The Congo Cookbook.

Glossary

ambassador—a high-ranking official sent by a country to represent its interests in another country.

arable—able to produce crops.

autonomous—politically independent and self-governing.

bonobo—a forest-dwelling chimpanzee of central Africa; it is smaller and more slender than the more common species of chimpanzee.

cabinet—a group of advisors who help manage a government.

cassava—a starchy tuber like the potato that is grown in Africa.

clan—a group of families that are descended from a common ancestor.

Cold War—a decades-long conflict between the United States and the Soviet Union that affected diplomatic relations between the allies of the two superpowers.

coup—the sudden overthrow of a government, usually conducted by the military.

decree—a command or order.

dictator—a ruler who has absolute powers to govern and to make laws.

export—the selling of goods to other countries.

gourd—the dried shell of a fruit that can be used as a container.

gross domestic product (GDP)—the market value of all the goods and services produced in a country.

headwaters—the streams that make up the beginnings of a river.

hydroelectricity—electricity generated by means of water pressure.

immigrant—a person who comes to a new country to live.

import—to bring merchandise or goods into a country from another country.

interim government—a temporary government put in place while a permanent government is formed.

literate—able to read and write.

nationalist—relating to a movement in which a people desire independence from a foreign power.

plantain—a topical plant, similar to a banana.

ritual—an established practice, often as a part of a ceremony.

savanna—a plain with coarse grasses and scattered tree growth.

secede—to formally withdraw membership from a state or country.

sedentary—remaining in the same area throughout the year and not migrating.

tributary—a stream that flows into a larger body of water.

Project and Report Ideas

Posters and Reports

Create a timeline charting the era of Belgian colonial rule in Congo. Begin the timeline with Henry Stanley's expedition of the region for King Leopold II. Proceeding from that year, include other important dates and events, and finish with the year the Congolese gained independence from Belgium. Draw your timeline on a poster board and share it with your classmates in an oral presentation. For each date of the era, explain why it is important, how it changed the lives of the Congolese people, and how it still may affect them today.

On a poster board, draw a bar graph showing the differences between the three climate regions of the Congo and your local area. Use different colors of crayon or marker for each bar on the graph. On a sheet of paper, write or type a short paragraph about the reasons why the plants and wildlife are different in each of the four climate regions. Explain how the average rainfall factors into these differences. Attach your paragraph to the poster board under your bar graph.

Creative Projects

Review the cultural differences between the Luba, Kongo, Lunda, and Mongo peoples. While you are doing this, think about the problems that might occur when members of the four groups meet for the first time. On a piece of paper, answer the following questions: What kinds of difficulties would different peoples have in communicating with one another? Would they welcome the other groups into their homes? What would they want to trade with one another? Discuss your ideas with your classmates. Then divide the class into four groups corresponding to the ethnic groups. Together as a class, write a play that dramatizes what you found in your class discussions. Play the part of a member of one of the Congolese groups, and act out a situation in which the four groups get along, working out their potential problems.

Project and Report Ideas

Pretend that you are Henry M. Stanley and you are walking through the Kongo rainforest for the first time. Take notes and answer the following questions: What kinds of new and interesting things might you see? What kinds of animals, birds, reptiles, insects, and plants? Be sure to include all the new sights, sounds, and smells you think you would encounter. Next, write a short story about your adventure, describing your feelings as you venture into a new and strange place. Share your report and story with your classmates.

The Congolese and other African peoples remember their African heritage by celebrating the holiday of Kwanzaa. If you could make up any holiday, what would it be? Would you name a holiday for yourself? Would you have everyone in your city or state celebrate your birthday? How would you celebrate the new holiday? What kinds of foods would people eat? Would they attend a parade? What else? In two or three paragraphs, inform your community of all the things it would need to know about it, including the following:

- date
- purpose of the holiday
- representative symbols or colors
- foods, games, music, and anything else that would honor the day

Chronology

10,000–1000 B.C.	Bantu-speaking people from West Africa migrate to the Congo region.
A.D. 700–1000	Other peoples migrate to the Congo and introduce hunting and farming.
1400s	The Luba Empire is founded and organized under one Luba king.
1482	Portuguese explorers, led by Diogo Cão, reach the Congo River and meet the Kongo people for the first time.
1500s–1600s	Europeans become heavily involved in African slave trading.
1874–77	Henry Morton Stanley explores the Congo River.
1878	Stanley helps settle the Congo for King Leopold II of Belgium.
1884	King Leopold claims the Congo region; names the new country the Congo Free State.
1908	The government of Belgium takes control of the Congo Free State away from King Leopold and renames the colony the Belgian Congo.
1956	Abako, an association led by Joseph Kasavubu, publishes a manifesto demanding that the Congolese be granted self-government.
1959	Rioting breaks out in Léopoldville in opposition to the colonial government.
1960	The Belgian Congo gains independence from Belgium; Kasavubu is named president and the first constitution is ratified; Patrice Lumumba is named prime minister.
1965	General Joseph-Désiré Mobutu launches successful coup and becomes president.
1967	Mobutu creates a new constitution that gives him all powers to rule and removes autonomy from the provinces.

1971	Mobutu changes the name of the country from the Congo to Zaire, along with changing the names of cities and regions.
1990	Mobutu allows new political parties to form; opposition to the dictator's rule increases; Mobutu appoints a transitional government.
1992	National conference creates a new constitution, but Mobutu does not recognize its authority; his government and the transitional government compete for control.
1994	Civil war in Rwanda leads to the deaths of an estimated 800,000 Tutsis and moderate Hutus; Hutu extremists escape to Zaire.
1996	Tutsi rebels take control of much of eastern Zaire.
1997	Anti-Mobutu forces and Tutsi rebels unite to capture Kinshasa in May; rebel leader Laurent-Desiree Kabila forces Mobutu out and takes over government; the country is renamed the Democratic Republic of the Congo.
1998	With support from Uganda and Rwanda, rebels advance on Kinshasa; forces from Namibia, Zimbabwe, and Angola intervene for Kabila and the Congo government; rebels are repelled but take control over much of the eastern region.
1999	The Congo and five other countries of the region sign the Lusaka peace accord.
2001	Laurent-Desiree Kabila is killed, possibly by his own bodyguard; Kabila's son, Joseph Kabila, becomes president.
2002	Joseph Kabila signs peace agreement with rebels in April.
2003	A new constitution is signed; an interim government is established that shares power with rebel leaders.
2004	Kabila promises to continue promoting peace in the Congo; the new presidential elections, first scheduled to take place in 2004, are moved to 2005.
2005	The government trains soldiers to help with the delayed election.

75

Further Reading/Internet Resources

Hochschild, Adam. *King Leopold's Ghost: A Story of Greed, Terror, and Heroism in Colonial Africa.* Boston: Houghton Mifflin, 1999.

Kushner, Nina. *Democratic Republic of the Congo.* Milwaukee, Wis.: Gareth Stevens Publishers, 2001.

Wamba, Philippe. *Kinship: A Family's Journey in Africa and America.* New York: Dutton/Plume, 2000.

Wrong, Michela. *In the Footsteps of Mr. Kurtz: Living on the Brink of Disaster in Mobutu's Congo.* New York: HarperCollins Publishers, 2002.

Wyanden, Jo, and Nina Kushner. *Welcome to the Democratic Republic of the Congo.* Milwaukee, Wis.: Gareth Stevens Publishers, 2002.

Travel Information

http://www.journeymart.com/DExplorer/Africa/DRCongo/default.asp
http://www.africaguide.com/country/zaire/

History and Geography

http://www.atlapedia.com/online/countries/DemRepCongo.htm
http://www.infoplease.com/ipa/A0198161.html
http://www.bartleby.com/65/co/Congo-Kin.html

Economic and Political Information

http://www.gksoft.com/govt/en/cd.html
http://lcweb2.loc.gov/frd/cs/zrtoc.html

Culture and Festivals

http://www.congo-pages.org/congoart.htm
http://www.congo-pages.org/livingbdd.htm

Embassy of the Democratic Republic of the Congo
1800 New Hampshire Ave.
Washington, DC 20029
(202) 234-7690 or (202) 234-7691

Congo-Kinshasa Permanent Mission to the United Nations
866 United Nations Plaza, Room 511
New York, NY 10017
(212) 319-8061
http://www.un.int/drcongo

U.S. Department of State
Bureau of Consular Affairs
Washington, DC 20520
(888) 407-4747 or (313) 472-2328
http://travel.state.gov

Index

Numbers in **bold italic** refer to captions.

Index

Contributors/Picture Credits

Professor Robert I. Rotberg is Director of the Program on Intrastate Conflict and Conflict Resolution at the Kennedy School, Harvard University, and President of the World Peace Foundation. He is the author of a number of books and articles on Africa, including *A Political History of Tropical Africa* and *Ending Autocracy, Enabling Democracy: The Tribulations of Southern Africa.*

Rita Milios is author of more than two dozen books for children as well as several books for adult readers, including teacher workbooks. Several of Ms. Milios' children's books have been translated into Spanish. In addition to writing, Ms. Milios is a practicing psychotherapist and a consultant to the education field. She lives in Toledo, Ohio, with her husband. She has two grown children.